ATTENTION-DEFICIT HYPERACTIVITY DISORDER

MENTAL ILLNESSES AND DISORDERS

Alzheimer's Disease
Anxiety Disorders
Attention-Deficit Hyperactivity Disorder
Autism Spectrum Disorders
Bipolar Disorder
Depression
Disruptive Behavior Disorders
Drug and Alcohol Dependence
Eating Disorders
Obsessive-Compulsive Disorder
Post-Traumatic Stress Disorder
Schizophrenia
Sleep Disorders

MENTAL ILLNESSES AND DISORDERS
Awareness and Understanding

ADHD
ATTENTION-DEFICIT HYPERACTIVITY DISORDER

H.W. Poole

SERIES CONSULTANT

ANNE S. WALTERS, PhD

Chief Psychologist, Emma Pendleton Bradley Hospital

Clinical Associate Professor, Alpert Medical School/Brown University

MASON CREST

Mason Crest
450 Parkway Drive, Suite D
Broomall, PA 19008
www.masoncrest.com

MTM Publishing, Inc.
435 West 23rd Street, #8C
New York, NY 10011
www.mtmpublishing.com

President: Valerie Tomaselli
Vice President, Book Development: Hilary Poole
Designer: Annemarie Redmond
Copyeditor: Peter Jaskowiak
Editorial Assistant: Andrea St. Aubin

Series ISBN: 978-1-4222-3364-1
ISBN: 978-1-4222-3366-5
Ebook ISBN: 978-1-4222-8567-1

Library of Congress Cataloging-in-Publication Data
Poole, Hilary W., author.
  Attention-deficit hyperactivity disorder / by H.W. Poole.
     pages cm. — (Mental illnesses and disorders: awareness and understanding)
  Includes bibliographical references and index.
  ISBN 978-1-4222-3366-5 (hardback) — ISBN 978-1-4222-3364-1 (series) —
ISBN 978-1-4222-8567-1 (ebook)
1. Attention-deficit hyperactivity disorder—Juvenile literature. I. Title.
  RJ506.H9P675 2016
  618.92'8589—dc23
                                    2015006700

Printed and bound in the United States of America.

First printing
9 8 7 6 5 4 3 2 1

TABLE OF CONTENTS

Key Icons to Look for:

Words to Understand: These words with their easy-to-understand definitions will increase the reader's understanding of the text, while building vocabulary skills.

Sidebars: This boxed material within the main text allows readers to build knowledge, gain insights, explore possibilities, and broaden their perspectives by weaving together additional information to provide realistic and holistic perspectives.

Research Projects: Readers are pointed toward areas of further inquiry connected to each chapter. Suggestions are provided for projects that encourage deeper research and analysis.

Text-Dependent Questions: These questions send the reader back to the text for more careful attention to the evidence presented there.

Series Glossary of Key Terms: This back-of-the-book glossary contains terminology used throughout the series Words found here increase the reader's ability to read and comprehend higher-level books and articles in this field.

People who cope with mental illnesses and disorders deserve our empathy and respect.

(istockphoto/digitalskillet)

Introduction to the Series

According to the National Institute of Mental Health, in 2012 there were an estimated 45 million people in the United States suffering from mental illness, or 19 percent of all US adults. A separate 2011 study found that among children, almost one in five suffer from some form of mental illness or disorder. The nature and level of impairment varies widely. For example, children and adults with anxiety disorders may struggle with a range of symptoms, from a constant state of worry about both real and imagined events to a complete inability to leave the house. Children or adults with schizophrenia might experience periods when the illness is well controlled by medication and therapies, but there may also be times when they must spend time in a hospital for their own safety and the safety of others. For every person with mental illness who makes the news, there are many more who do not, and these are the people that we must learn more about and help to feel accepted, and even welcomed, in this world of diversity.

It is not easy to have a mental illness in this country. Access to mental health services remains a significant issue. Many states and some private insurers have "opted out" of providing sufficient coverage for mental health treatment. This translates to limits on the amount of sessions or frequency of treatment, inadequate rates for providers, and other problems that make it difficult for people to get the care they need.

Meanwhile, stigma about mental illness remains widespread. There are still whispers about "bad parenting," or "the other side of the tracks." The whisperers imply that mental illness is something you bring upon yourself, or something that someone does to you. Obviously, mental illness can be exacerbated by an adverse event such as trauma or parental instability. But there is just as much truth to the biological bases of mental illness. No one is made schizophrenic by ineffective parenting, for example, or by engaging in "wild" behavior as an adolescent. Mental illness is a complex interplay of genes, biology, and the environment, much like many physical illnesses.

People with mental illness are brave soldiers, really. They fight their illness every day, in all of the settings of their lives. When people with an anxiety disorder graduate from college, you know that they worked very hard to get there—harder, perhaps, than those who did not struggle with a psychiatric issue. They got up every day with a pit in their stomach about facing the world, and they worried about their finals more than their classmates. When they had to give a presentation in class, they thought their world was going to end and that they would faint, or worse, in front of everyone. But they fought back, and they kept going. Every day. That's bravery, and that is to be respected and congratulated.

These books were written to help young people get the facts about mental illness. Facts go a long way to dispel stigma. Knowing the facts gives students the opportunity to help others to know and understand. If your student lives with someone with mental illness, these books can help students know a bit more about what to expect. If they are concerned about someone, or even about themselves, these books are meant to provide some answers and a place to start.

The topics covered in this series are those that seem most relevant for middle schoolers—disorders that they are most likely to come into contact with or to be curious about. Schizophrenia is a rare illness, but it is an illness with many misconceptions and inaccurate portrayals in media. Anxiety and depressive disorders, on the other hand, are quite common. Most of our youth have likely had personal experience of anxiety or depression, or knowledge of someone who struggles with these symptoms.

As a teacher or a librarian, thank you for taking part in dispelling myths and bringing facts to your children and students. Thank you for caring about the brave soldiers who live and work with mental illness. These reference books are for all of them, and also for those of us who have the good fortune to work with and know them.

—Anne S. Walters, PhD
Chief Psychologist, Emma Pendleton Bradley Hospital
Clinical Professor, Alpert Medical School/Brown University

CHAPTER ONE

DISTRACTION

Words to Understand

deficit: a lack of something.

hyperactive: too active.

meta-study: an analysis of many scientific studies on the same subject.

overdiagnose: to determine more people have a certain illness than actually do.

For lots of kids, the day before summer break is their favorite school day of the year. Most teachers don't even try to teach anything on that day. They know that their students' heads are filled with visions of vacation. It would be silly to try and teach a difficult lesson on the last day of school. Who would be listening? Most kids are thinking about the trip they are going to take or the new Xbox game they're going to play, or they are just feeling happy they won't have to wake up so early anymore. Nobody wants to sit still and focus on a lesson.

We've all felt this way from time to time. We've all been excited the morning of a school field trip. We've all had trouble focusing on homework on the night before a big game, dance, or school play. But some kids feel restless, distracted, or excitable when there is no vacation or big game. Imagine waking up one morning with that feeling like it's the last day of school . . . when it's actually just another Wednesday in February. You can't sit still, or you can't stop

It's normal to be distracted sometimes, but too much distraction can make it hard to succeed in school.

AS AMERICAN AS ADHD?

In a 2012 editorial in *Psychology Today*, Dr. Marilyn Wedge declared that "French kids don't have ADHD." She argued that French parents have different expectations for their kids. As a result, far fewer kids have the "behavior problems" that American kids do.

Many people assume that ADHD is an American problem. This is partly because so many American researchers study the disorder. Some people also assume that the symptoms are cultural. That is, they think that *most* Americans are hyperactive with short attention spans. They might even joke that the entire country has ADHD.

But when researchers performed a **meta-study** of data from more than 100 countries, they learned something interesting. In most other countries, kids have ADHD-like symptoms about as often as American kids. Behaviors that are called ADHD in the United States might be viewed differently in other places. But the problems are still there. So while the term ADHD might be American, the symptoms are universal.

talking—but nobody seems to understand why. In class, let's imagine the teacher is giving you instructions on how to solve a math problem. Sounds easy enough. But as she explains the instructions, you start thinking about soccer practice and miss her explanation. This makes answering the problem almost impossible.

Kids who can't stay focused on a task are sometimes labeled as **hyperactive**. They may have ADHD, which is short for attention-**deficit** hyperactivity disorder. Kids with ADHD usually have trouble paying attention in school, but it's not just that. They also struggle with staying organized and following instructions. They can be forgetful and fidgety. Sometimes kids with ADHD have trouble taking turns. They can't seem to play quietly, even when they will get in trouble if they don't. They might be pushy or silly and not notice when their friends have had enough. Having ADHD can make it extremely difficult to succeed in school, and sometimes it can really affect friendships. Unfortunately, it is one of the most common mental disorders.

A Distracted History

The name ADHD is fairly new. But problems with attention and focus are not. In 1798, a doctor named Sir Alexander Crichton may have been the first to diagnose this medical problem. In a book chapter called "On Attention and its Diseases," he wrote about a problem that involved "the incapacity of attending with a necessary degree of constancy to any one object." Modern doctors now believe Crichton was talking about ADHD.

Over the years, various names have been used to describe the problems we now call ADHD. The different names reflect changing ideas about the nature of the disorder. In the 1920s, it was called "minor brain damage," because doctors believed that the problem was caused by some injury. We now believe that only a very tiny number of ADHD cases are related to a physical injury. (See chapter three for more about possible causes.)

DID YOU KNOW?

ADHD is the most common mental disorder among kids.

THE FIDGETS

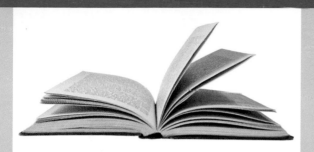

Here is more of what Sir Alexander Crichton wrote about attention problems:

In this disease of attention . . . every impression seems to agitate the person, and gives him or her an unnatural degree of mental restlessness. People walking up and down the room, a slight noise in the same, the moving a table, the shutting a door suddenly, a slight excess of heat or of cold, too much light, or too little light, all destroy constant attention in such patients. . . . They say they have the fidgets.

Later names for the disorder included "minor brain dysfunction" and "hyperkinetic reaction of childhood." In the 1980s, the term attention-deficit disorder was used. And by the end of the decade, the word hyperactivity had been added.

Modern ADHD

The number of kids diagnosed with ADHD has been steadily increasing in the 21st century. In 2003, 7.8 percent of American kids under 18 had been diagnosed with ADHD. By 2007, that number had gone up to 9.5 percent, and in 2011, about 11 percent of kids had been diagnosed. That's more than 6 million total, just in the United States.

One interesting thing is that the number of cases varies a lot in different states. In other words, ADHD diagnoses are increasing everywhere, but they are increasing at different speeds in different states. In 2011, Nevada had the lowest

STATES WITH LOWEST PERCENTAGE OF KIDS WITH ADHD, 2011	
State	**Percentage of kids with ADHD**
Nevada	4.2
New Jersey	5.5
Colorado	5.6
Utah	5.8
California	5.9
Alaska	6.0
Hawaii	6.0
New Mexico	6.2
Idaho	6.7
Illinois	7.2

STATES WITH HIGHEST PERCENTAGE OF KIDS WITH ADHD, 2011	
State	**Percentage of kids with ADHD**
Kentucky	14.8
Arkansas	14.6
Louisiana	13.3
Indiana	13.0
Delaware	11.7
South Carolina	11.7
North Carolina	11.6
Ohio	11.6
Iowa	11.5
Michigan	11.2

Note: Includes kids aged 4 to 17 who were diagnosed by doctors or reported as having ADHD by their parents.

Source: Centers for Disease Control and Prevention, "Trends in the Parent-Report of Health-Care Provider Diagnosis and Medication Treatment for ADHD: United States, 2003–2011." http://www.cdc.gov/ncbddd/adhd/prevalence.html.

percentage of kids with ADHD, while Kentucky had the highest. Researchers aren't sure why this would be. Many states with higher percentages were in the South and have high poverty rates. But Ohio, Indiana, Iowa, and Delaware—states with lower poverty rates—were also in the top 10. So it seems that geography or poverty is not the main cause. Maybe doctors in one state have a tendency to find more ADHD than doctors in other states. Maybe it has to do with the educational systems in different states. The situation is probably too complex to blame any one factor.

One problem? There is no formal test to determine whether a kid has ADHD. Questionnaires, called "rating scales," are widely used. They help doctors compare the attention and activity levels of a specific child to other children the same age. There are also computerized analyses that can help with diagnosis. But these assessments are up to the professional to use. The personal opinions and observations of doctors play a big role in diagnosing ADHD.

Finding the Cause

There are a number of theories about why this increase is happening. Some people wonder if certain environmental factors are causing more ADHD cases. Some foods and chemicals have been blamed, for example. On the other hand,

ETHNICITY AND ADHD

A study found that African American kids are 69 percent less likely to be diagnosed with ADHD than Caucasian kids. Hispanic kids are 50 percent less likely, and other ethnicities are 49 percent less likely to be diagnosed than Caucasian kids. Researchers wonder if cultural differences are responsible. In other words, do Caucasian families view certain behaviors as "problems" that families of other ethnicities do not?

That may be part of the reason. But another statistic is worrying. In the same study, the lack of health insurance was connected with fewer ADHD diagnoses. In other words, in populations where less health care is available, fewer kids are diagnosed with ADHD. This suggests some kids may not be getting help. Experts fear that minority kids with ADHD might not be getting the medical attention they deserve.

we may simply understand ADHD better than we used to. In other words, maybe there are not actually more kids with ADHD. Maybe we are just better at finding them.

Then again, some people argue that we are too good at finding them. In other words, they think that we **overdiagnose** ADHD. Some argue that we are too quick to label basic behavior issues as mental health problems. Other people worry that drug companies, which enjoy huge profits from ADHD medication, have convinced us to see ADHD everywhere.

But when kids' schoolwork, friendships, and families are suffering, it is hard to argue that nothing is wrong. While experts debate causes, the most important thing for families is to get the help they need.

If you are worried about ADHD, talk to your pediatrician.

Text-Dependent Questions

1. What are some of the former names for ADHD?

2. What are the theories about why rates have been increasing?

3. What are the three states with the lowest rates of ADHD? What are the three states with the highest?

 Research Project

Find out more about ADHD rates in different countries. Some countries have rates very similar to those in the United States, while others (such as France) have much lower rates. What cultural expectations might make it more or less likely for kids to be labeled as having ADHD?

CHAPTER TWO

SYMPTOMS AND TYPES

 Words to Understand

aversive: causing someone to want to avoid something.

inattention: distraction; not paying attention.

impulsivity: the tendency to act without thinking.

predominantly: mainly.

Not all people with ADHD behave in exactly the same way. There are different "flavors" of ADHD that result in different behaviors. But there are several aspects of the disorder that are common for most people. Let's look at the three categories of behavior, and then talk about how these can combine into different types of ADHD.

Inattention

One of the most common features of ADHD is what doctors call **inattention**. Examples of inattention are the following.

- failing to notice details
- making lots of careless mistakes; doing messy work

Boys are diagnosed with ADHD more than twice as often as girls. About 20 percent of boys in high school have been diagnosed with ADHD.

- difficulty finishing schoolwork or chores
- difficulty organizing tasks and activities
- disorganization
- often losing or breaking things
- being easily distracted
- not listening
- forgetfulness about daily activities
- difficulty following rules (even fun rules like in games)
- seeing complex tasks as **aversive**, or to be avoided

The tricky part is, everybody does these things sometimes. Inattention is a completely normal human behavior. The problem comes when the symptoms described above happen all or almost all the time.

You might get distracted in math class because you don't like math. But what if you like math just fine and get distracted anyway? Or what if you love basketball, but you keep making mistakes because you have trouble paying attention to the game? This is one reason ADHD is such a big problem. The disorder keeps kids from doing things they *need* to do, like homework, and things they *want* to do, like sports (or whatever hobbies they love).

Hyperactivity

Another very common feature of ADHD is hyperactivity. Examples include:

- fidgeting or squirming
- tapping hands or fingers; shaking legs or feet
- not staying seated when expected to
- running or climbing when told not to

Opposite: Sports require mental focus, which can be hard for kids with ADHD.

- difficulty playing quietly
- talking too much

Just like inattention, these behaviors are no big deal if they only happen sometimes. They happen to everybody sometimes! Hyperactivity becomes a problem when it interferes with daily life.

Impulsivity

The third category of behaviors is called **impulsivity**. Examples of impulsivity include:

- blurting out answers before questions are finished
- difficulty waiting for one's turn
- interrupting other people
- starting conversations at wrong times
- grabbing objects from others
- clowning around
- actions that may lead to accidents
- frequent impatience

ADHD AND OTHER DISORDERS

The behaviors associated with ADHD can also be symptoms of other problems. For example, anxiety and depression can make kids seem very distracted. And there are many disorders, such as bipolar and conduct disorders, that involve impulsive behavior. Even physical illnesses can cause some of the same symptoms.

Some experts worry that parents and teachers can be too quick to assume a child has ADHD. It's important to carefully explore all aspects of the problem with a mental health professional before jumping to conclusions.

Because kids with ADHD have trouble controlling their impulses, they may have trouble sticking to a healthy diet. Studies have shown a link between overeating and ADHD.

Types of ADHD

The examples listed above are all symptoms of ADHD. But not every person has all of those symptoms. That's why ADHD diagnoses come in several types. Which type a person has depends on whether his or her symptoms are **predominantly** related to inattention or to hyperactivity and impulsivity.

- **Predominantly inattentive**. The majority of symptoms are from the inattentive category, with little or no symptoms from the hyperactivity or impulsivity categories.

- **Predominantly hyperactive/impulsive**. The majority of symptoms are from the hyperactive and impulsive categories
- **Combined**. The symptoms are equally split between all categories.
- **Other specified**. The person has a variety of symptoms, but not enough to qualify as any of the other three types.

ADHD can also be considered mild, moderate, or severe. This depends on two factors: (1) how many symptoms the person has, and (2) how badly the symptoms interfere with daily life.

To diagnose ADHD, doctors often use forms called rating scales, where they note how often a particular behavior occurs. A typical rating scale will ask questions along these lines:

Does the patient:
1. make careless mistakes with homework?
2. have trouble staying "on task"?
3. not listen when spoken to?
4. get distracted easily?
5. fidget with hands or feet?
6. have trouble playing quietly?
7. have trouble taking turns?
8. interrupt people frequently?

Then the parent, teacher, or patient responds with: "very often," "often," "occasionally," or "never." In the list above, the first four questions relate to inattention, questions five and six relate to hyperactivity, and seven and eight relate to impulsivity. Through these questions about different behaviors, mental health professionals can determine what type of ADHD someone has and how severe it is.

Text-Dependent Questions.

1. What are the three main categories of ADHD behavior?
2. What are some examples of each?
3. What are the broad types of ADHD that people can have?

Research Project

Find a rating scale for ADHD online and try to group the questions into the symptom categories mentioned above: inattention, hyperactivity, and impulsivity. Rating scales are available online from various sources, such as the website of Children's Hospital at Vanderbilt (http://www.childrenshospital.vanderbilt.org/ uploads/documents/DIAGNOSTIC_PARENT_RATING_SCALE(1).pdf).

CHAPTER THREE

CAUSES OF ADHD

Words to Understand

correlation: a relationship between two things.

edible: something that can be eaten.

genes: the elements in cells that determine what traits we have.

neurotransmitters: brain chemicals that transmit impulses from one nerve to another.

toxin: poison.

With rates of ADHD increasing, people are eager to understand what causes the disorder. Unfortunately, there is probably no single cause. Instead, researchers think that a number of factors combine to create ADHD symptoms in certain kids and that the causes can vary from kid to kid.

Physical

Chapter one pointed out that ADHD used to be called "minor brain damage." The name was changed because it was not an accurate description of the disorder. However, in a tiny number of cases, ADHD may have been caused by an injury to the front part of the brain. This injury could have occurred before birth or soon after. But, again, this only applies to a very small number of cases.

THINGS THAT MIGHT LOOK LIKE ADHD

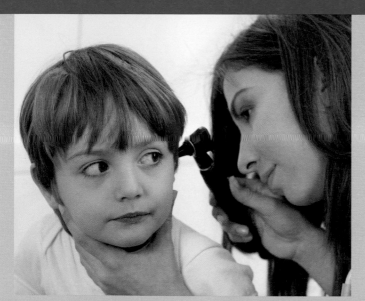

A doctor will need to rule out physical problems that might cause symptoms that are similar to ADHD.

Before diagnosing someone with ADHD, a doctor will want to rule out the following:

- vision problems
- hearing problems
- ear infection
- anxiety or depression
- learning disability
- any other medical problem that could cause inattention or hyperactivity

Another possible cause is if a mother smoked cigarettes while she was pregnant. But this theory needs more study before it is proven. We do know that women who smoke have a higher chance of having kids with ADHD. However, people with ADHD are more likely to smoke. This means that while smoking and ADHD are related (scientists call this **correlation**), one might not cause the other.

Genes and Chemistry

Let's imagine a woman who is a smoker and who has ADHD. She becomes pregnant, and because she knows that smoking

Researchers use technology like this MRI scanner to study the brain. They are trying to figure out if the brains of people who have ADHD are different from those who don't have ADHD.

is bad for her baby, she quits. But the baby might end up having ADHD anyway. That's because ADHD may have a genetic cause, making it possible for the disorder to be passed from parents to children.

Scientists have identified a few different **genes** that may have a connection to ADHD symptoms. However, there does not seem to be one single gene that is responsible. It is more likely that something goes wrong in the interactions between various genes.

Researchers studied the brains of some kids with ADHD, and they discovered something interesting. Although the kids' brains were normal—there was no injury, for example—parts of their brains developed more slowly than in kids who don't have ADHD. Researchers found about a three-year delay in brain development, but only in certain parts of the brain. More study is needed before we can know for sure what this discovery means.

DID YOU KNOW?

About one-third of parents who had ADHD as kids will have kids who also have ADHD.

Another research area has to do with the chemistry of the brain. Chemicals called **neurotransmitters** in the brain pass messages back and forth to each other. Problems with the production of those chemicals might contribute to ADHD. Many other disorders, including depression, anxiety, and bipolar disorder, may also be caused by problems with brain chemistry. The brain chemical called dopamine seems to be involved in all these problems, and it probably plays a role in ADHD, too, along with a few other neurotransmitters.

Lead used to be added to paint because it helped make the paint last longer. But inhaling or ingesting lead can interfere with brain development. Lead paint was banned in 1978, but it can still be found on many old buildings.

Environment

Environmental causes of illness come in two different forms. Sometimes *environment* refers to an exposure to particular **toxins**. For example, many years ago, lead was used in paint, gasoline, and water pipes. We now know that lead can cause problems with brain development. It is possible that exposure to lead over a long time might result in ADHD. Other researchers have suggested that certain pesticides, which are used in food production, could have the same effect.

The word environment can also refer to the way someone lives. Sometimes people call this *lifestyle*. When people blame ADHD on too much television or on bad parenting, they are saying that the environment of the child caused the disorder.

TURN OFF THE TV

It used to be common to blame ADHD on watching too much television. Researchers thought they had found a relationship between lots of TV and behavior problems at school. Further studies have found that while TV is definitely not an ideal activity, it is probably not a direct cause of ADHD. Still, doctors agree that limiting TV and other "screen time" will benefit your overall health and help you do better in school.

In some countries, such as France, many people believe that the home environment is the cause of most child behavior problems. The American view, on the other hand, is that the environment only has a limited role in mental disorders. American doctors do agree that parents can learn to build better environments for their children. However, most of them dispute the French idea that the parenting causes the problems in the first place.

The Sugar Debate

For a long time, people believed that foods with a lot of sugar in them caused ADHD. In a way, it's easy to understand why this would be. Sugar is basically **edible** energy. When a person eats a lot of sugar, he or she might seem more active, or even hyperactive. It won't last very long, because the body burns up sugar quickly. But sugar and sugary foods do provide energy for short periods. So if a little sugar makes you active, it seems likely that a lot of sugar would make you hyperactive.

But here's the thing. Science doesn't care about what "seems" true. Science is the search for what is actually true.

To test the sugar theory, scientists designed a study. A group of kids were given food containing a sugar substitute called aspartame. The scientists then told half the parents that the food had no sugar, only aspartame. But they told the other half that the food did have sugar.

Many parents find it hard to believe that sugar does not directly cause hyperactivity! But science has not been able to prove the two are connected.

From this, the scientists learned something very interesting. The parents who *thought* the food had sugar reported more hyperactivity. It turned out that the sugar content of the food was less important than the parents' beliefs about the food.

So while it seems obvious that sugar causes hyperactivity, the current science tells us that this connection may have more to do with our perceptions than with reality.

But even if food doesn't cause ADHD directly, diet probably can make symptoms better or worse. In the next chapter, we will talk about various things people with ADHD can do to feel better. A healthy diet is definitely on that list.

Text-Dependent Questions

1. What are some of the main theories about the causes of ADHD?
2. What is the difference between a cause and a correlation?
3. What do scientists believe about sugar's relationship to ADHD?

Research Project

Find out more about the different theories of what might cause ADHD. Make a list of proposed theories and write down what evidence you find. What theories make the most sense to you?

CHAPTER FOUR

TREATING ADHD

 Words to Understand

carbohydrates: substances in food, such as sugar and starch.

elimination: complete removal of something.

stimulant: something that increases energy or interest.

Depending on how severe it is, ADHD can be treated with medication, therapy, or a combination of both. But most mental health professionals believe that a combination is the most effective treatment.

Medication

The most common drugs for ADHD are **stimulants**, which are sold with names like Ritalin and Adderall. Since stimulants can make people more energetic, it might seem strange to treat a hyperactive person with a stimulant. However, these particular stimulants act on the parts of the brain that control focus and attention. Doctors think that by helping the person become more focused, stimulants help the person also become calmer.

People with untreated ADHD are at increased risk of developing drug and alcohol problems. Research has shown that treating ADHD with stimulants can help reduce that risk.

The medications come in liquid and pill forms. Stimulants affect each person a bit differently, so doctors will frequently adjust the type and amount of drug a few times before finding what works best. There are other drugs beyond stimulants that also can help kids with ADHD.

Although drug therapy is not a magic cure, it can offer concrete help—and real hope—to the thousands of children and their parents who experience these disorders. Each individual is different and needs to be evaluated by a professional to determine the best treatment.

SIDE EFFECTS

Like all drugs, medicines for ADHD also have side effects. People should be aware of possible problems and report them to their doctors as soon as possible.

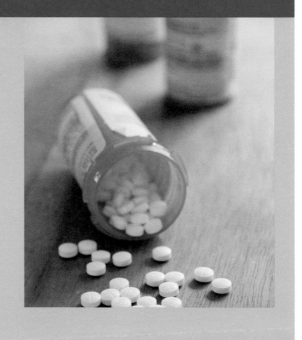

- **Reduced appetite.** Some kids who take stimulants lose weight—sometimes a great deal of weight—because they are not hungry. Parents and doctors should be aware of the child's ideal weight and make sure it does not drop too low.

- **Insomnia.** Taking stimulants can also make it difficult to get a good night's sleep. Again, it's important to talk to a doctor if this problem occurs. Things can be done to help, such as changing the dosage or the time the medicine is taken.

- **Suicidal thoughts.** This is a rare side effect, but it does happen, both with stimulants and other forms of ADHD medication.

DISTRACTED DRIVING

Distracted driving is a problem for most people. But it is even more of a problem for people with ADHD.

Teenagers with ADHD are involved in four times as many car accidents as kids who don't have ADHD. That's why treatment is so important. It's not just about schoolwork; it's about safety, too.

Therapy

In addition to medication, behavioral therapy can also be very helpful for kids with ADHD. In this type of therapy, kids learn new skills to help them get along better in school and with friends. For example, kids who tend to be impulsive might practice waiting their turn or sharing their toys. Other kids might practice interacting with other people. For example, they might learn to watch the other person's expression and then respond in a useful way.

Some parents of kids with ADHD also attend therapy. Classes in parenting skills can help moms and dads learn now to use a more positive form of discipline. Kids with ADHD tend to get a lot of negative feedback and criticism. Experts believe that it is important to give positive feedback—praising kids when they do pay attention, complete tasks, or remember to wait their turn. It is also important to help children have positive experiences somewhere. If school always is a problem, then kids with ADHD need some other activity—such as sports, drama, or music—that can help them feel good about themselves.

There are also support groups, websites, and organizations for parents of children with ADHD. Talking with others who have similar struggles can be helpful.

Diet

Chapter three discussed researchers' discovery that sugar is probably not a cause of ADHD. There are no studies proving that food colorings or pesticides cause ADHD, either. However, that does not mean that diet has no role to play.

First, some kids—not all, but some—really do react to sugary foods. Other kids may be sensitive to certain chemicals added to food. So while these substances probably do not *cause* ADHD, they might make some kids' symptoms worse.

Good sources of protein include meat, fish, eggs, cheese, yogurt, nuts, and seeds.

Doctors believe that protein helps some ADHD medicines work better. A diet that is high in protein (meat, eggs, beans, cheese) might help reduce symptoms. Meanwhile, eating fewer simple **carbohydrates** (sugar, white rice and flour, potatoes) could also be useful. And omega-3 fatty acids (found in olive oil, some nuts, and some fish) are also known to be good for health.

Most mental health providers advise a well-rounded diet with all the food groups included. And they warn against super-strict **elimination** diets. An elimination diet involves removing certain foods from the diet in order to have a certain effect. For instance, "gluten free" is a very popular form of elimination diet. (Gluten is a substance in wheat that is in many foods, including baked goods and pastas; some people blame gluten for various health problems.) There's nothing wrong with experimenting a bit, to see if changing your diet makes you feel better. For example, a kid with ADHD might try cutting out sugar for a week, just to see if he or she feels calmer. But doctors and caregivers should be consulted before making any major diet changes, especially eliminating entire groups of food.

Strict elimination diets can be risky because they rule out so many options. As mentioned, most medications given for ADHD are stimulants, which tend to make kids less hungry. So it's especially important that kids on medicine have complete, healthy meals when they do eat. Many parents find that kids who take medication may not eat much for lunch. So, eating

DID YOU KNOW?

If you have ADHD, you might want to avoid foods that have:
- sugar
- artificial colors (brightly colored cereal, candy, or frosting)
- caffeine

a good breakfast (before taking the medicine) and a healthy dinner (once it wears off) are both very important.

If You Have ADHD . . .

The challenges of ADHD —inattention, hyperactivity, and impulsivity—are not easy to live with. But with time and patience, it is possible to manage the disorder. Here are a few tips to help make life a bit easier.

- **Stick to a schedule.** Try to do the same things— getting up, washing, getting dressed, eating breakfast—at the same times every day. Routines can seem boring at times, but they really do help you stay on track.

- **Get organized.** Create clear, uncluttered spaces and have a place for everything. Use homework organizers (file folders and so on) to keep your school work in order.

- **Take care of yourself**. Remember to eat healthy meals and get enough sleep. Find a physical activity you enjoy and try to do it often. These basic things can do a lot to make you feel happier and more in control of life.

- **Ask for help**. Find adults and friends you can trust, and let them help you. Many schools have special programs for kids with problems like ADHD.

- **Explore new activities.** Kids with ADHD might find some activities more difficult than others. Individual sports—running and other track sports, for example— might be easier to handle than team sports. Or, an instrument like the piano, which can be played solo,

Opposite:
Being active, which could mean joining a team or simply having fun outside, is a good way for kids with ADHD to burn off extra energy.

might be better than a band-focused instrument. The point is, don't stop looking for outlets that work for you.

- **Praise yourself.** It's very easy to get stuck thinking about what you've done wrong. Try to notice what you do right. Maybe you were in class and really wanted to get up and walk around the room, but you chose to stay seated because you knew that's what your teacher wants. You have every right to be proud!

Text-Dependent Questions

1. What type of medication is most commonly used to treat ADHD?
2. What are the side effects?
3. What else can people with ADHD do to manage their disorder?

Research Project

Find out more about ADHD support in your area. What are the resources in your school, town, county, or state that families with ADHD might be able to use?

Further Reading

BOOKS

Nadeau, Kathleen G., and Ellen B. Dixon. *Learning to Slow Down and Pay Attention: A Book for Kids about ADHD.* Washington, DC: Magination Press, 2004.

Quinn, Patricia O. *Attention Girls!: A Guide to Learn All About Your AD/HD.* Washington, DC: Magination Press, 2009.

Shapiro, Lawrence E. *The ADHD Workbook for Kids: Helping Children Gain Self-Confidence, Social Skills and Self-Control.* Oakland, CA: Instant Help Books, 2010.

Taylor, John F. *The Survival Guide for Kids with ADD or ADHD.* Minneapolis, MN: Free Spirit Publishing, 2006.

ONLINE

Kids Health. "ADHD." http://kidshealth.org/teen/diseases_conditions/learning/adhd.html.

National Institutes of Mental Health. "What Is Attention Deficit Hyperactivity Disorder (ADHD, ADD)?" http://www.nimh.nih.gov/health/topics/attention-deficit-hyperactivity-disorder-adhd/index.shtml.

PsychCentral. "Childhood/Teenage Attention Deficit Disorder." http://psychcentral.com/disorders/childhood-adhd.

LOSING HOPE?

This free, confidential phone number will connect you to counselors who can help.

National Suicide Prevention Lifeline

1-800-273-TALK (1-800-273-8255)

"Mental illness is nothing to be ashamed of, but stigma
and bias shame us all. Together, we will replace stigma
with acceptance, ignorance with understanding, fear with
new hope for the future. Together, we will build a stronger
nation for the new century, leaving no one behind."
—Bill Clinton

Series Glossary

acute: happening powerfully for a short period of time.

affect: as a noun, the way someone seems on the outside—his attitude, emotion, and voice (pronounced with the emphasis on the first syllable, "AFF-eckt").

atypical: different from what is usually expected.

bipolar: involving two, opposite ends.

chronic: happening again and again over a long period of time.

comorbidity: two or more illnesses appearing at the same time.

correlation: a relationship or connection.

delusion: a false belief with no connection to reality.

dementia: a mental disorder, featuring severe memory loss.

denial: refusal to admit that there is a problem.

depressant: a substance that slows down bodily functions.

depression: a feeling of hopelessness and lack of energy.

deprivation: a hurtful lack of something important.

diagnose: to identify a problem.

empathy: understanding someone else's situation and feelings.

epidemic: a widespread illness.

euphoria: a feeling of extreme, even overwhelming, happiness.

hallucination: something a person sees or hears that is not really there.

heredity: the passing of a trait from parents to children.

hormone: a substance in the body that helps it function properly.

hypnotic: a type of drug that causes sleep.

impulsivity: the tendency to act without thinking.

inattention: distraction; not paying attention.

insomnia: inability to fall asleep and/or stay asleep.

licensed: having an official document proving one is capable with a certain set of skills.

manic: a high level of excitement or energy.

misdiagnose: to incorrectly identify a problem.

moderation: limited in amount, not extreme.

noncompliance: refusing to follow rules or do as instructed.

onset: the beginning of something; pronounced like "on" and "set."

outpatient: medical care that happens while a patient continues to live at home.

overdiagnose: to determine more people have a certain illness than actually do.

pediatricians: doctors who treat children and young adults.

perception: awareness or understanding of reality.

practitioner: a person who actively participates in a particular field.

predisposition: to be more likely to do something, either due to your personality or biology.

psychiatric: having to do with mental illness.

psychiatrist: a medical doctor who specializes in mental disorders.

psychoactive: something that has an effect on the mind and behavior.

psychosis: a severe mental disorder where the person loses touch with reality.

psychosocial: the interaction between someone's thoughts and the outside world of relationships.

psychotherapy: treatment for mental disorders.

relapse: getting worse after a period of getting better.

spectrum: a range; in medicine, from less extreme to more extreme.

stereotype: a simplified idea about a type of person, not connected to actual individuals.

stimulant: a substance that speeds up bodily functions.

therapy: treatment of a problem; can be done with medicine or simply by talking with a therapist.

trigger: something that causes something else.

Index

Page numbers in *italics* refer to photographs.

About the Author

H. W. POOLE is a writer and editor of books for young people, such as the *Horrors of History* series (Charlesbridge). She is also responsible for many critically acclaimed reference books, including *Political Handbook of the World* (CQ Press) and the *Encyclopedia of Terrorism* (SAGE). She was coauthor and editor of the *History of the Internet* (ABC-CLIO), which won the 2000 American Library Association RUSA award.

About the Advisor

ANNE S. WALTERS is Clinical Associate Professor of Psychiatry and Human Behavior. She is the Clinical Director of the Children's Partial Hospital Program at Bradley Hospital, a program that provides partial hospital level of care for children ages 7–12 and their families. She also serves as Chief Psychologist for Bradley Hospital. She is actively involved in teaching activities within the Clinical Psychology Training Programs of the Alpert Medical School of Brown University and serves as Child Track Seminar Co-Coordinator. Dr. Walters completed her undergraduate work at Duke University, graduate school at Georgia State University, internship at UTexas Health Science Center, and postdoctoral fellowship at Brown University. Her interests lie in the area of program development, treatment of severe psychiatric disorders in children, and psychotic spectrum disorders.

Photo Credits

Photos are for illustrative purposes only; individuals depicted in the photos, both on the cover and throughout this book, are only models.

Cover Photo: iStock/monkeybusinessimages

Dollar Photo Club: 13 vvoe; 15 Gelpi; 16 michaeljung; 19 rimmdream; 23 BlueSkyImages; 27 andrecastock; 31 Jacek Chabraszewski; 32 Frédéric Prochasson; 35 Monkey Business; 36 JJAVA; 37 mario beauregard ; 38 a4stockphotos; 40 Mat Hayward. **iStock.com:** 10 pixdeluxe; 11 phillipimage; 21 McIninch; 30 gwflash. **US Navy:** 28.